THE

INGREDIENTS
YOUR
BUSINESS
NEEDS
TO
SOAR HIGH

Josef O. SEAN

Contents

Terms and Conditions

Legal Notice

In practical advice books, like anything else in life, there are no guarantees of income made. Readers are cautioned to rely on their own judgment about their individual circumstances to act accordingly.

This book is not intended for use as a source of legal, business, accounting or financial advice. All readers are advised to seek services of competent professionals in legal, business, accounting and finance fields.

Dedication

This project is dedicated to Almighty God the creator of the universe. (Yahweh Borie)

INTRODUCTION

S

uccess is one colorful thing the world runs after from inception of existence, the pursue of success does not necessarily portray competition is involved, the point is no one like to be seen as a failure; not because failure has been tasted to be sore but celebration of success if always awesome.

Whatever instance or situation where success could be noticed, failure could as well be recognized therein. This implies success and failure are immutable things, having either of them is determined by lot of factors. The way at which these issues of life are handled also determines the result of a generated reaction.

Everyone on planet earth desire success and wants to be celebrated, but the sad side is sometimes people just want it without wanting to pay the price for it. It's even argued that many don't even know the basic price for success; well that's a discussion for another day.

A successful situation is considered to be when your activities bring you fulfilling joy; this is often referred to as a win-win situation.

Your activity as it concerns this eBook is what we call Business.

What is a business? Who owns or manage a business? What are the things associated with business activities? Sorry about this, this book is for those who already know answers to all these! This eBook would be using few words in some kind of proverbial way.

The process, through which a business is conceived, researched about and formulated plus the strategic involvement and implementation of its activities could be referred to as cooking.

Practically cooking involves the use of ingredients and style, while style includes timely decisions and actions, ingredients are those factors put in place for a business to be in operation.

Ingredients are known to enhance nicest smell, delicious taste and body needed nutrients.

The success of every business is determined by the inputs of the handler (entrepreneur, business owner or manager) these inputs includes variable factors of production, the fixed production factors, timely decisions and actions, mentorship advice or model followership guidelines and most importantly optimistic and well wishing mindset including prayers.

Take this or leave it: Every successful business in the physical world has a successful spiritual side, which is attained by some level of sacrificial input depending on which ever means seems pleasant to the business owner or handler.

Aside following the basic rules of life with relation to business, the spiritual side is also important. Prayer and spiritual activities have a way it affects life, it is left to you as a business owner or handle to ascertain which works best for you among all spiritual means known. Just ensure the positive side of your spirituality does not cover up your eyes from whatever consequences it may also come with. Meanwhile one can get a spiritual means whose yields have no negativity at all.

A small mathematics here: considering the number line, you would recur we have the plus side to the right and the negative signs to the left with the centre- ZERO. If the number line is used to measure one's spirituality level, the farther you are from zero the higher your wealth of connection to the powers at both end. Standing on the fence with no action means remaining with zero.

This is the most dangerous point in business, waiting for luck, luck doesn't come to those who do not take action, be a risk taker and ensure to take positive actions.

This eBook will be detail about practical ways to ensure the success of a business, maximizing the best out of every available ingredient to ensure growth and success in business.

The success of a business can only be measured through Sales.

WHERE DOES SALES EMANATE FROM?
Where are the sales? That's the question when a loan marketer approaches any Trader for loan; especially a rational business-person. Only few know it takes rounds of turnover for a business to pay back a loan conveniently without affecting the business equity.

The stability, sustainability and success of any economy is determine by sales, no matter how productive a nation or a firm is, if the sales segment remains sluggard, then productivity must at one point diminish...Well some other factors involve.
Let's leave that and just talk about sales!
Okay... Am really interested in discussing this too, there are few basic things needed to put in place for   effective   sales.
Permit me get started with the first few ones in the introductory part of this eBook, subsequently others will be reviewed.

You need to have a sellable product - if your major products are stuffs that are not needed often then what you need do is get complements (accessories) of such major products and add them to your stock and watch what happens.

There is a difference between making sales and outshining your competitors.

Examine this- You can make sales that aren't enough for you to plunge back into the business after incurring your daily expenses, if this continues perpetually the working capital would definitely get a big blow.

In a slow Economy, profit is determined by a high level of turnover (accumulation of little profits) profits builds wealth.

The necessity and drive to make sales at a level that accommodates basic and the unnecessary luxury expenses, as well as outshining competition is the primary motive behind the extra mile quest for spirituality.

(My advice) choose your spiritual means wisely.

There would be various practical samples discussed to help grab the basic things as it may concern each business.

CHAPTER ONE:

DEFINING A PURPOSE

A

buse is inevitably when the purpose of something is lost or not known. A business without a purpose has a hundred percent likelihood to get stuck and halt operations. Its stop may or may not be in form of liquidation; it may just be that the roadmap hits a road block due to shortage of means.

Being aware that the business world calls for different strategic endeavors; the first step in beginning a transformative effort that can ignite long-lasting, positive change and bring about growth in business, is to define the purpose of your business. So business owners or managers must respond to this challenge and define the purpose of being in business; this can be achieved by *identifying and understanding the reasons behind the creation of your business.* This serves as what motivates and spurs every action and steps to be taken as regards the progress and success of your business.

If you are starting a new company or reinstating an existing one, you need to *define your purpose* or reason for running the business. You need to be clear about why you're in business in the first place, what direction the business is heading and what exactly you want to get out of it.

Generally, people see the primary purpose for a business to be financial but being unsatisfied when working for someone else had trigger the mind of many to kick start a business. The need for more money or wealth is another cogent reason why people start a business- that's the desire for *an independent income*.

Trust me, **independent income** is far more preferred than what anyone else is willing to pay you, though independent income is determined by your own ability to succeed and excel in the marketplace.

Starting a business in a slow economy has its own inherent risks. People who are confident in their ability to handle their own affairs are often happier when running their own businesses, even with increased risks, responsibilities and stress but they are in control. Yes! They have control over their time, they could decide to go for vacation or have a rest, which may not be convenient or permitted when you work for someone.

Some businesses got started because the owner enjoys being involved in things which are passionate to him; this type of entrepreneur gets fulfilled with excitement of activities in the market place rather than profits.

Some businesses are founded primarily for the purpose of serving a particular environment. A non-profit business is a dedicated one for the poor, and perhaps the disadvantaged and those stricken by disaster, profit oriented businesses also provide useful and essential services to the public, they may only combine purpose which is serving the community with what they need and using that privilege to garner their profit. A good example is a grocery store which ensures the supply of good food to surrounding residents hence providing a decent living for its owner. This interprets the point where self-interest intercepts community service.

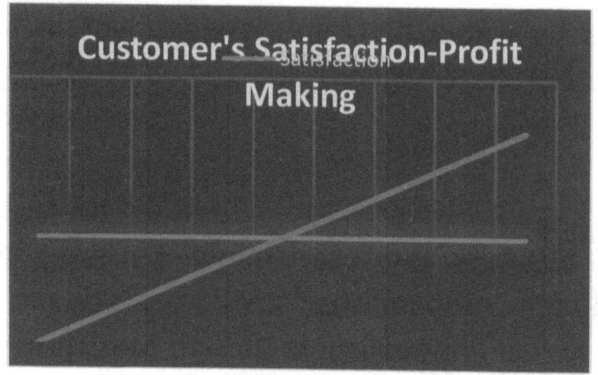

You can be in a particular business owing to the passion you have for such business; you can be in business because of your favored access to some particular resources. You can also be in business because you discover the environment you find yourself needs a particular stuffs; you key into that to make it available, most times this is always a boom especially if your purpose of being in business includes profit making!

Purpose inspires and stimulates the workers of an organization, helping them tailor their effort towards a common goal or objective. Purpose is long-term and focuses on visible results. It is belief-driven, though bigger and wider than the organization's goods or/and services, yet in line and reverberate its values.

A business purpose should be brief but clear, direct, motivational and inspirational; it must be actual and realizable though most times it requires arm-stretching efforts and hard work to make it actualized.

Defining purpose is very different from mission statement, the later actually is made ready such that it can tell what you want to achieve with the means and steps to get them achieved.

Purpose on the other hand tells who you are as an organization and answers the question; why you do what you do?

Purpose is given support by a vision, mission and core values. Together, these essential components provide a road map that is focused and guided, and they give meaning to the organization's specific actions and undertakings.

CHAPTER TWO

IDENTIFY THE LEVEL YOU EXPECT FOR YOUR BUSINESS

You are reading this book because you sensed your business is not already at the level you want it to be. Sure-bet you got a business running just that it keeps struggling for growth or its growth has been thwarted by several forces in the business world.

This book is not prepared to review or teach the theoretical approach of business, this book is not going to be concerned with theorems formulated by Business College professors who were never in business, this book will address how the modern day business operates with regards to obtainable issues and practical situations encountered on the field of play for different businesses and how to thrive under any circumstance.

Your purpose of being in business remains a major determinant in attaining the level you want for the business.

This chapter will be of immense help to those whose interest in business is for wealth creation and excellence in name.

To be assured of making your business become a household name, earn a high level of integrity that registers your business name in the mind of people (especially when services that relates to what your company offers come across peoples' mind or become the topic within a gathering), then they are lot of works to be done.

No one can teach you how to know the level of success you want for yourself or business, it has to come from within. The drive for success comes from within, this will help you pay the sacrificial prices when necessary without being cajoled or pushed.

To properly identify the level expected of your business, three cogent questions must be answered...

i.   Where are we?
ii.
iii.   Where are we going?
iv.
v.   How shall we get there?
vi.

For success driven business persons, identifying the level you want for your business starts from identifying the current level of that very business and comparing it with that level you want to attain and itemizing the difference. *The difference is what you need to work on.*

This difference then becomes your target; this difference becomes your next line of action and operations. Be mindful this difference needs to be worked on with a time frame; there must not be a rush. Strategically set out the roadmap for achieving this difference, you need to plan on how you can improve to get a better version of this '*difference*'.

Ensure to make a different 'difference' to make you standout, when you difference outshines others then your business becomes a model for others.

To work on achieving the difference in your current level of business and your 'to be' level of business, it is essential to strategically plan in line with the organization's vision and mission statements. This will help to monitor the progress of your organization and ascertain success.

The expected levels could be based on the following categories:

- Finance
-
- Customer service
-
- Number of Employee
-
- Image and Reputation
-
- Sales and marketing.
-

You must be certain of the level your business has attained with reference to certain factors or departments in the organization, to do this; you could employ the SWOT (strength, weakness, opportunities and threats) principle to access and examine both the internal and external happenings and then you put down the changes and works that must be done to help reach the targeted level.

When you don't raise the bar per time to ensure your business attain the level at which you wish it could be, the best you could hope for is just a maintenance of the present status quo and if there arises challenges that could destroy or significantly damage the reputation and image of the organization then you fall back to point zero, therefore it is expedient to never settle in the present level.

To attain the level you want for your business, you must work with the right set of minds, right set of employees or workers, always finish what you started, have strategic meetings where the mind is passed to every member of the organization, be disciplined and take continuous action.

It's important for a business that wants to grow to have expectations of level they want to operate or reach in certain time range or period. This will challenge employees to put in required considerable efforts.

Kindly watch the video on this link...

https://www.linkedin.com/feed/update/urn:li:activity:6437642309646454784

Kindly copy and paste link into address bar on your browser.

You should answer the following questions to arrive at your expected level: In a number of years let's say Three, Five, Seven or Ten...

- ✓ What will the world look like?
- ✓
- ✓ What will be the important trends affecting my line of business?
- ✓
- ✓ What will our line of business be dealing with and what would it look like?

- ✓
- ✓ What will be our image?
- ✓
- ✓ What will our customers be saying about us and why will they remain loyal to us?
- ✓
- ✓ What will we be doing that no one else will?
- ✓
- ✓ How big will our organization be? How many employees will we have?
- ✓

Planning like this will give room for you to run growth assessments. You therefore should get accustomed and expectant of several different possibilities. This should help you plan and then narrow your focus from the present state to addressing what needs to be done and put in place both for the immediate growth and for the level you wish to attain in your business.

CHAPTER THREE

CHOOSING THE RIGHT MODEL FOR YOUR BUSINESS

Among the most difficult transitions for many persons, is moving from being an employee to an entrepreneur. The idea of having your own business and being your own boss is simply mind-blowing. Along with this thrill comes certain strategic issue that must be addressed upfront if your business is to succeed in the long run.

Quite a number of people started a business without the consideration of things like choosing the most suitable model.

It is really crucial that you pay attention to your Business Model as it could make the difference between a successful business and a failed venture. The principle to be discussed applies, whether you are running your business online or offline. Every successful business was built around a sound business model, not around a revolutionary product or idea. I'm not trying to pull your legs....You will soon find out why.

SO WHAT EXACTLY IS A BUSINESS MODEL?

You may have attempted getting into the entrepreneurial field in the past but regrettably, you were not able to pull through unlike some other successful people. What made the difference? One matter cutting across all types of businesses which made them successful is - *they have the right business model.*

If you have attended business school or some management courses, you may already be familiar with the term Business Model.

A business model is more than just your product idea.

For sake of simplicity, we will define a business model as *"The rationality behind how your organization creates, delivers and captures value."*

As an entrepreneur, it is your job to define what value you want to deliver to your target audience (buyer). It could be economic, social or otherwise....*it's your duty to decide!*

You won't be great at being an entrepreneur until you are able to define what value you want to deliver and how you are going to do this effectively. Having a great idea is not enough to succeed. Any great idea needs a great business model.

THE BUSINESS MODEL CANVAS

An essential but easy to use tool that will aid you in choosing the right model for your business is the Business Model Canvas (BMC). The BMC is a visual tool with 9 key elements that will help you:

- Understand the essential elements needed for your startup to succeed.
-
- Monitor your progress.
-
- Identify the key points to emphasize when pitching your idea to investors.
-

- Clearly define the customer segment your business is addressing.

-

- Identify your Unique Value Proposition to each customer segment.

-

- Define the channels through which you will communicate these value propositions to your customers.

-

- Identify how you will establish and maintain relationships with your customers.

-

- Clearly identify your different revenue streams and pricing strategy.

-

Business Model Canvas Template

Below is a sample Business Model Canvas Template showing the nine key elements or building blocks. It's now your job to fill in the necessary information which will help to clearly define your business model. At first sight, this may seem like a daunting task. However, as you familiarize yourself with the BMC, you will be able to fill in all required elements.

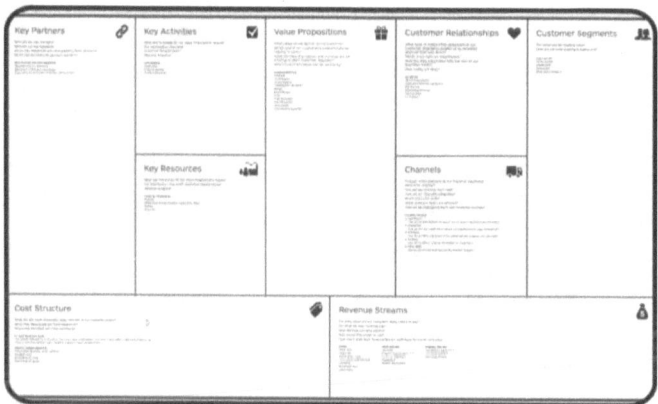

It isn't Just About Having "The Right Product"

One of the biggest and most common mistakes made by entrepreneurs, particularly those just starting out on their entrepreneurial journey, is focusing narrowly on creating an **_ideal product._**

For many tech startups, this is a grim reality. Sometimes, there is so much focus on "Technology" that other aspects of the business are ignored and when the product is finally ready to launch, they fail woefully because of failing to communicate with the marketing team or other departments in order to understand what the market truly wants. While building an innovative product is great, it is equally important to back that product up with the right business model, lest all your efforts fizzle out after a short while.

For your budding venture to blossom into the business of your dreams, you need to keep testing until you find the right model that suits your customers. Remember, it's not all about you. So ideally, you should make sure your communication is right; your pricing is right, as well as your channel of delivery to your target customers.

Getting your business model right requires a lot of testing and discipline. Trying to be everything, all at once would only result in one thing – failure of your venture. In most cases, many venture capital firms would insist that the technical aspects of the business and the strategic aspects be handled separately and by separate individuals. However, the two roles must work hand-in-hand to get things right.

If you take a careful look at successful businesses, you will discover one thing in common - they took their time to validate their idea or prove the business model before taking off in full steam. In the same way, you are going to test every element of your business model to determine the best fit for your customer segment. For example, you may need to work on your pricing to know what your customers prefer or can afford.

Take, for a sample, do your customers prefer to pay for your services as a monthly subscription or can they afford a full-blown stand-alone package? In order to establish this, you may need a couple of beta testers as a case study and then determine from their feedback what best approach to adopt.

Here are a few steps that would help you establish the right model for your business:

Try to gauge the value you are bringing to your customer segment: Your products (solution) should solve your customer's problems rather than give them more headaches. *If it does that, perfect!*

Also, you need to estimate your production costs and place a reasonable markup to establish your price. Consider the prevalent market price for similar products and services as you set your own prices. Set your price too high and you risk losing your customers. In the same way, setting your prices too low will leave you bankrupt or being considered inferior.

Locate an aspect of your pricing and delivery which will make you remain competitive yet attract customers more.

Envisage and appreciate feedbacks: Now that your product prototype is ready, it is time to get customers to try it out and gauge their user experience from their feedback. From their responses, you will be able to tell if your product and services makes their life easier or you need to go back to the drawing board. If the latter is the case, then it is pointless working on your business model.

Study how your channel works in real life: In order to do this, you will need to work with a selected group of customers. They will tell you if your product was easy to access or not, as well as the best route of communication. It was said that Fred Smith first mailed a parcel to himself in order to test the FedEx business model and see how efficient the overnight delivery service of FedEx was. You can do something similar too.

Getting testimonials from your customers: endeavor to be very close to the first few customers who accessed your business. Ask them for their sincere testimonials which you can publish on your website or review sites. This can work wonders for your business. If they are skeptical able providing positive testimonials for your business, this may be a bad sign for you.

Design a small and localized rollout plan: A cost-effective way to test your business model is to do so in your local community and with a select but diverse group of customers. With a limited budget, you can test and tweak some elements of your business model like pricing, distribution channel and cost before going full steam or before expanding your inventory.

Establishing the right business model takes a lot in terms of time, energy and resources whether your business is online or offline. Sufficient effort should be put into establishing the model as you also did while developing your service or product. You have to be prepared to test and tweak every element of your business model until you arrive at something that is scalable and sustainable.

WHY DO YOU NEED A ROLE MODEL IN BUSINESS?

Attaining heights requires following some fundamental principles, so is having and running a successful business. One prominent rule of life is having a role model, it helps you guide yourself with a kind of laid down pathway, you learn from the mistakes of your role model and try to improve on other areas at which your role model faltered.

As a business owner, you should have an eye for greatness; you need to picture your business to be as great as the existing key players in the industry you operate.

Set Goals that scares you and at the same time excites you.

Watch and study the industry and select one of the topmost firms as your model, especially after watching and discovering your company and this company share similar attributes and values.

You need to start working with a strategic plan which enable you tread on the same pathway this big company trod, ensure this is done without imitation. Instead, find a way to improve on what serves as strength to the organization, analyze your role model's weakness and see how to mitigate around and get better with that. ***Then the business becomes a boom!***

The effective handling of top industry players' weakness by creating a palatable situation around what they have negative ratings for, will definitely earn your business the accolades that will announce its name and integrity, thereby building up value.

Let's have this practical explanation....

It was a rainy day in a city called AK, fortunately electric Power supply was on, this is a rare situation, as the country was a developing country. Joe was engrossed in the world cup match going on as it was the month for the prestigious tournament, yet he needed to visit the barbing shop before late as people roll-in in numbers to barb at night. Going at night will make him leave his pregnant wife at home for too long.

He eventually got up and set for the barber's shop with an umbrella, after having a nice cut, he suddenly remembers he needed to withdraw cash at the ATM stand and buy few groceries needed at home. On getting to the road side he waved down a cab which he boarded straight to the e-Banking centre nearest to him. After withdrawal, he crossed to the shopping mall opposite the road to get the needed items and move to the road side to get a cab back home.

Due to the rain the cabs were being filled up from afar, so he accosted a Bike-Man and this ensued:

Joe: Hello

Bike-Man: welcome, where do I take you to?

Joe: AG crescent before united schools

BIKE-MAN: 100 bucks

Joe: no its 50 bucks

Bike-Man: you can see its raining; I can't ride out in the rain for 50 bucks...

(Never underrate any customer)   **(Meanwhile the rain was only drizzling)**

Joe: ok thanks (left him and move forward)

Bike-Man: come let's go

On the way the Bike-Man reported a fellow Bike-Man to Joe, he went away with my passenger before you arrived, I don't think I can forgive him. Joe asked why?

He replied: I already told the woman one hundred and fifty bucks and she agreed, then the other guy beckoned on her, telling her he can do it for seventy bucks that was how the woman left me for him....

Abnormal or excessive profit may damage your business, be prudent when giving out prices. The Bike-man Joe hired was the vice chairman for bike riders association in the environment, but he couldn't use his high name to make sales. The other guy worked on the vice chairman's weakness (He likes too much profits) and he won the sale tussle.

Joe: but sir, the fair should be fifty bucks not one hundred and fifty bucks?

Bike-Man: Yes, but its rainy-more so we are the ones who fixed the price at fifty we have the right to adjust it due to the situation on ground.

Another Bike-Man drives past and called Bike-Man carrying Joe his boy

Bike-Man carrying Joe replied am richer than you, I should be the one calling you my boy (He was seriously furious).

Moral lesson as shared by Joe: *Don't see yourself as too big or too rich to neglect small sales and small profits. The big wealth of today is an accumulation of small but consistent profits. When this huge wealth is expressed by being spent and there is no replacement, it's a sign that being broke is about to happen!*

CHAPTER FOUR

SETTING BUSINESS GOALS

So you've got a great business, awesome! Have you thought about where you would love your business to be five years from now? That is a question many business owners would rather put off. After all, we do not know what tomorrow would bring, or do we? While that may seem like a logical conclusion, the truth is every business needs a clearly mapped out direction. Running a business without clearly mapped out strategy is like walking blindfolded in a desert and without a compass.

Many of us are home-based entrepreneurs and we tend to avoid Goal setting and time management because we love the freedom of working at home. For a long time, some of us fought planning and scheduling. It is only until we gave up that fight that we started getting everything done and having extra time to do what I wanted. We wrongly thought that planning and goal setting and all those other time management skills would tie us down and stifle our creativity.

If you are like many online entrepreneurs you seem to be doing a lot of work and piling up the projects to the point of overload without seeing profitable results. You have all these training programs, you're buying all these products, software, you are setting up website after website. If that sounds like you, it's really time to stop what you're doing and assess your business goals.

What are goals?

Every one of us has one goal or the other. Some of them are quite stellar in nature (for example becoming the CEO of a Fortune500 company at the age of 24) while others are relatively mundane, like losing 10 pounds over a period of one month. Whatever our goals are, there must be some valid reasons for setting such goals or so we suppose. In addition to personal goals, there are also business or corporate goals. In effect, there is no single "ideal" definition of what a goal is. However, we would like to give a broad definition of the term for sake of simplicity.

One source defines a goal as: "The desired result envisioned by a person or a group and accompanied by an effort aimed at the achievement." This definition includes all the major elements which make up a goal, namely: (a) the desired result (b) a vision (c) effort/commitment.

This implies that simply daydreaming about building a million dollar business isn't a goal. You need to get off your couch and actually plan how you are going to achieve that and also take necessary actions to see it come true. As once stated by the popular motivational speaker Jim Rohn "Action completes the miracle."

Goals and Objectives: What's the difference?

In business or management parlance, there is usually a distinction between goals and objectives. In reality, both concepts are related and yet separate in some ways. It is a common saying that goals without accompanying objectives are unachievable, while objectives without goals will lead to stagnation. So it is essential to use both if you want to achieve your personal or business goals.

Management experts usually tell us that goals are our final destination while objectives are the various steps or progress made in order to arrive at our destination. In other words, goals are the long-term outcomes while objectives are the smaller chunks or actions needed to achieve these outcomes. Objectives tend to be more specific and short-term in nature. Additionally, goals tend to be broader in nature while objectives are single actionable points that aid in achieving the overall goal, be it business or personal.

Are all goals reasonable or realistic?

In the true sense, there is no such thing as an "unreasonable" or "unrealistic" goal. Our goals define who we are and are often guided by our belief system. One of the shortcomings of many persons and organizations is trying to define their goals according to society's standards and expectations. Social perceptions should not be a measure employed in 'validating' the reasonableness or unreasonableness of a personal or business goal.

History has proved time and again that many of the great ideas which have helped to shape our world were once laughed at and considered unreasonable. This is because those who the ideas were shared with either did not fully comprehend them or thought they were unachievable. No wonder the famous life coach, Les Brown once said: "Many people fail in life not because they aimed too high and miss but because they aimed too low and hit." That basically sums it up. In all honesty, there is no goal that is unreasonable. When you set a goal, define it by who you are, your personal conviction and objectives, and not by anyone else's belief.

There is a popular story of an engineer and a philosopher. The engineer proposed building a ship from metals, and insisted that the ship would float. The philosopher looked at him in the face and without a word, dropped a piece of metal in a container of water that was right in front of them and the metal immediately sank to the bottom of the container. Without a doubt, the idea of building floating ships out of metals sounded ridiculous back then. But today, we know better.

The above example and others prove that all goals and objectives are valid, no matter how strange they may appear. So don't be discouraged from aiming high or dreaming wide because of public opinions. If you can visualize it, you can achieve it.

How to Set SMART goals

If you've ever attended a management or business class, you will often be told not only to set goals but make sure they are SMART. What exactly does it mean to set "SMART" goals? The word SMART is actually an acronym for

S - Specific

M - Measurable

A– Attainable (or Ambitious, in some quarters)

R - Relevant

T–Time-bound

In order to make your business goals SMART, it is important to consider your organization's mission statement and then align your goals with it. Your organization's mission statement should be memorable and concise, inspiring you to do only the things that are in line with the direction your organization is headed and away from less important things.

For instance, if your organization's mission is to be the foremost Marketing Company in your local area or county, then the goals you set should be in line with developing your organization's marketing capabilities. Areas like social media marketing should be given attention to. Other forms of media marketing should also be considered as you build your strategy around dominating the marketing space.

Remember that SMART goals need to be specific, measurable, attainable, relevant and time-bound. So, if you are a business owner, you must ensure that you set goals that are truly representative of the measurable results you need to achieve in your business. On the other hand, if you are hired as a manager for a firm, you will need to set goals that help create value for your unit.

Next, it is essential you convert each strategic output into a measurable objective that your business should achieve within the year. These objectives are specific tasks or areas of improvements that the business should record within the year. As an entrepreneur it is your responsibility to consult with your team in order to ensure everyone is in consonance with your company's long-term mission. In this way, they are clear about what they are expected to achieve within the year.

Why you should set SMART goals

By setting the right goals and objectives, you will be able to point your business in the right direction, ensuring that it remains on track at all times. SMART goals tell you WHERE you want to go while objectives tell you HOW you will get there. The table below is a useful tool that will help you keep track of your goals and setting

GOALS	Improve the businesses visibility	Reduce the number of late orders

reasonable metrics. The example in the table will help you with an idea of how to use this simple but awesome tool.

When your business is able to achieve its set goals, you'll then be able to clearly link your performance to your role as the manager, and to the overall success of the organization. This will help you to clearly bring value to your clients and scale up your business over time.

TIMELINES	Within the next 6 months	Within the next 3 months
OBJECTIVES		
1.	Create a new awesome logo	Employ additional hands
2.	Put up Signage at the store	Purchase automated equipment
3.	Create an ecommerce website	Implement an online ordering system

CHAPTER FIVE

ACTION PLAN – STRATEGICALLY UTILIZING THE AVAILABLE TO MAXIMIZE PROFITABLE SALES

If you have bought this eBook, you must have been so curious about the details needed to be known from you to shoot your sales to the topmost level you desire or project.

With the effective practice of the rudiments in this chapter and eBook in total, you are assured of a *catapultive* movement of your sales and turnover level to a height you might never have imagined.

I will like to start with by stating that you business does not just exist, grow and stay healthy with sales. Sales are in different forms, there are sales on credit, which may run down a business venture, there are sales without profit too; which often occur when there is an urgent need of money when the owner lacks funds; he might need the money to meet up a loan repayment, personal or family expenses or even operational expenses.

I have witnessed situations where sellers sell their products at cost prices or less, even you might have done that before.

THE SALES EVERYONE LOVES

That's the sales with instant payment plus huge or normal profit at the least. Every seller at one point in time has experienced this and loved it, its frequency is what is now coveted and prayed for. This kind of sales is what builds up wealth, not the kind of sales that forces you to spend your working capital as low sales has made you broke. Once this is dominant the business may crash if care is not taken.

The love and desire for the regularity of good sales triggers the essence of spirituality in business.

To be candid the first thing to settle in business is your spiritual connectivity with whatever you believe in, ceteris paribus, once all other things are intact you are guaranteed maximum patronage.

The next big thing is your product, if your product is not the next big thing or the next needed thing then you may struggle with sales. Earlier in this eBook i stated how to combine everyday needs with sale of items that are purchased seldom-ly.

From research consumables are the most purchased products, people keep buying because they need more as soon as the previous one is used or consumed.

If you do not sell products that could be purchased often, then add accessories to your stock and watch your sales.

CAPTURING SALES FROM FAR AND WIDE

Some businesses are established to serve a locality, while we have businesses whose terrain and dominance are felt far and wide, such are the big companies around today.

These big companies do a lot of things the small businesses cannot do, they spend so much on advertisement and endorsement contracts with celebrities.

If I own a small business, I will invest on branding and strategic marketing.

Location Matters: factors surrounding the perfect choice or decision about the location of a business are much as well as very important; in deciding the location of a business, there is the need to consider things such as easy access and availability of the materials needed for it to function well, but most importantly, the nearness of finished products' location to the people who needs and will be buying these end product or services.

If by any means, your business is located distant from those who needs its products or services, then the three things to do are:

I)   Ensure you run awareness programs

II)

III)   Ensure to get a show room or outlet close to those who needs your products or services, where order and delivery can be made and processed.

IV)

V)   Ensure to integrate technology into your business operations and how it can be accessed.

VI)

Moreover, distance is never a barrier when the heart really finds love or undiluted satisfaction for a product or for its seller.

What makes people leave other sellers in the neighborhood for their preferred seller in a far location? Most times it does not necessarily depend on price, at times it's determined by the rational desire for **VALUE** and the preferential treatment accorded to them by these sellers at the far end.

Ensure to present value, then people will find you from any location, location is paramount, if you are too far from where you can be easily accessed then get an outlet to a good location where clients can see what you have in gallery or exhibition and can be directed to the main warehouse or production location.

BRANDING AND MARKETING: This element is discussed into details in the next chapter owing to the fact that it serves as one of the prominent action to be taken in any strategic Sales oriented plan.

Once there is a sell-able product which carries the value people need, then the next big step is ensuring to package it (products and services) in a unique way that makes it not only pleasing or enticing to the eyes and heart but also make it poses a unique look that will make it stand out among others.

The act of aggressive one on one prospection has been long abandoned by many marketers, whereas this is the soul of marketing, no advertisement process can answer all questions and clear doubts in the mind of prospects like one on one prospection. Though some business operation may not find this permissive, in this case cold calling and emails can be employed. It should be noted that your customer service team has to be excellently efficient in attending to clients and prospect.

TRENDY MEANS OF MARKETING IN RECENT DAYS ARE AS FOLLOWS:

Email Marketing: a company can either hire an email copywriter and marketer on freelancing sites or acquire the software(s) needed and right personnel to operate it. A well written 'awareness' and 'captivating' content is composed and sent as email to a large number of emails. Trust me you have some of these kinds of mails in your inbox. Consider sending something of such about your business to one million people at a go! At the worst you will get a reasonable percent contact you back for inquires and patronage.

Social Media: The social media has been the most trendy activity based medium recently, with millions of uses using different platforms on daily basis, your business is guaranteed of receiving attention when it's been showcased there. The most popular is Facebook; you can run Facebook ads to a target audience selected by geographical location as well as interest with minimal charges that can be increased as time goes on based on result derived. There are also other means that can be used on different social media platforms, get acquainted and enjoy the benefits.

Press Release: press release are powerfully written to create awareness about products and services through the media, you can get this done by professionals on freelance sites and see the result.

INTEGRATING TECHNOLOGY INTO BUSINESS OPERATION IS CONCERNED WITH USING WHAT IS IN VOGUE TO YOUR FAVOR.

The world has become a single village with the advent of technology especially the **INTERNET**. Using the internet to your favor should be the idea to develop more on daily basis.

*Your website is your online office, if you don't have a website yet, you business may limited or confined to your locality. Read about **'FIND MY BUSINESS ON GOOGLE'** to discover this secret.*

Having a website comes with various other packages that could fetch you money depending on your type of business, if you are into digital products you can have a blog section which also permits an Ad-sense account, traffic on your website will not only fetch you sales but also some cool cash from Google.

The Impetus to continually make profitable sales and keep your business soaring high at a geometric progression rate, you get started with having a sell-able product or catchy service, ensure to be strategically located, equip the business with the right personnel and needed machineries, create awareness to the world at large using various possible means, then you need an excellent team of customer relations officer to seal up every sale deal, if not the whole effort before clients contact your business becomes futile.*(details in customer relation chapter).*

CHAPTER SIX

UNDISPUTED VALUE OF MARKETING AND BRANDING

Like I said earlier on, this eBook would be focused on Street-smart business methods of making sales rather than the theoretical theorems propagated and taught in business schools and colleges. This is not to rubbish the orthodox economics, business studies and schemes learnt while in school but rather, it's to help put to practice and identify how to adjust to the trend of the current situation.

In this chapter we would be considering the undisputed value of Marketing and what it entails as well as the place and importance of branding.

Marketing is an extremely important activity that determines the survival and success of any business. The marketplace of today has experienced the ugly side of slow economy and one sided activity especially sales. This prompts lot of companies resulting in hiring marketing personnel and setting crazy targets with a motivational clause and pay of huge commissions as benefits. In same vein people gets fired when they do not meet sales target overtime.

Having a team of marketers is not just the determinant to the success of a business venture but there is the need for business owners and managers to ensure a functional and efficient marketing strategy is put in place.

Many business owners believe marketing is all about better quality products and services presented at competitive rate by their hired promoters or marketers. Marketing cannot be said to be effective when prospects are not converted to clients (make purchase). Consistent profitable sale is that one thing every company will do anything to have.

Sales oriented marketing is better achieved with street smart techniques. Marketing requires being tactically skillful, being resilient, aggressive with optimism, excellent with interpersonal relationship, knowledge-able about the strength and uses of your products and versed to analytically convince people's heart. Marketing involves magnetic friendliness. Unfriendly marketer will never win a prospect not to talk of converting a prospect into leads or client.

MARKETING IS TACTICALLY AGGRESSIVE IT REQUIRES RESILIENCY:

How ideal is forcing people to buy your products, no matter how qualitative and value-able it is? As a marketer, your aggressiveness is built in the mind. You should be solidly optimistic; this drives you to your goal. A marketer needs to be mindfully aggressive and believe making sales is nothing but a possible and a must do task. Never take **'NO'** for an answer, ensure to reach declining prospects over and over again. What would be your reaction? When you as a marketer get engage with a prospect in a sales situation and he or she tells you: "Let me think about it, they can mean a lot of things they're not telling   you."

In most cases, some people will take that as a "No. I'm not interested at this time".

If you care to know: I will think about it means I want to digest this details (seed) you just gave me, it means you as a marketer needs to water the seed by doing follow up.

You can get CRM software or keep proper records of your prospects' contact and check on them regularly as they may turn to be a client later on.

An abandoned prospect may get info of another product (substitute) marketed by another seller at a later time; he may decide to go for it, with the mind that he needs it now. *Your follow up strategy and schedule is key; it's the only sure thing to help out.*

As a marketer you need to understand there would definitely be some obstacles to be overcome in meeting people out there. It's also not just about giving you attention and listening to you but getting interested in what you say. You have to find a catchy way to make you presentation. The secret here is first you need to be attractive. *Be nicely dressed, identify and stick to the nicest level of dressing you can afford.*

Accosting a prospect may not be easy, as a marketer you need to be bold to present your product. There are often few people out there who are ready to counter your products from the weak side of the products, this implies you need to understand the strengths of your products and versed with great comments to counter any negative remark. Marketers may face being chased out or booed. Never get pissed off; hence you need to be tactically skillful especially in the area of human relation. You need to be excellent with interpersonal relationship skills.

TECHNOLOGY AND MARKETING: HOW IT'S COMBINED

Technology has been proved to be of immense help in virtually all areas of life. The use of technology in relation to marketing has been tested and very helpful, it basically focuses on creating awareness to people who needs or may need your products and services. Marketing is more of communication, without communication, marketing can never be efficient. To this end the present day communication and attention catching elements are used in capturing peoples' attention towards various products and services. Let's consider the following:

Marketing via **THE INTERNET** is one of the most effective and prominent means in recent days. With *Facebook ads* you can get your product and services advertised to targeted audience whose interest is about your products or products relating to yours as being registered and saved on the Facebook's database.

Have you heard of **Business Whatsapp** or **Whatsapp Sender Pro**? It's a cool app to monitor you business and send bulk messages to lots of people, they get to know about what you can offer and whoever is interested contacts you back, it's cool to operate.

Google is your friend, with the new feature called **'Find my business on Google'** *internet* users searching for products and services that relates to your business get a list of businesses in their nearest location displayed to them, they in turn get contact details of whichever business seems suitable. Imagine being call for supplies by clients who gets your contact on Google just like that!

Have you tried **LINKEDLN,** learnt a cool lesson on LinkedIn on one of my vacation days, a friend whom we just got connected buzzed me and sent a welcome message which was accompanied with the values he can offer, got trilled, I developed that skills by search for people who may need what I have too on social media, I joined groups whose interest in what I have determines their existence, then I let out the dog from the bag, I let them know I can offer them a particular service or products they may need and t a very considerable price and turnaround time....in three months, it became a boom!

I guess you should try this trick on any platform you find yourself.

Your **WEBSITE** is your online office or business location, you will agree with me that lots of shopping stores today with website has increased their sales with the shopify or ecommerce feature, lots of business with websites has enhanced features that permits order to be placed online as well as delivery. Today virtually all things can be ordered online without visit to physical showrooms or outlet. Get a website today, run ad-sense and wait to see the increased awareness enjoyed by your company.

With the aid of technology, customized messages about a product can be sent in form of email or short message service (SMS) to a great list. Email marketing uses lead generation while bulk SMS can be done through SMS websites after acquiring phone directories, which is often sold based on categories such as location, occupation and interest.

Instagram bot is another great tool that can be employed, though some class of the society claims it's not really in vogue as it used to be, but I assure you it still work wonders. Instagram bot is a circle of Instagram users coming together as a group and each member is responsible to like and comment other members post, hereby drawing attention of the public, you and I know a post with massive comment is always captivating to the eyes. Learn more about IG bots and use it to your favor.

Marketing promotes a brand yet a brand is bigger than any marketing strategy or attempt. A brand remains even after the marketing effort has swept through the room. A brand is what sticks in the mind when your organization, product or services is mentioned or remembered.

There are various schemes that can be exhibited to be a marketing strategy, one effective one is ***promotional campaign.***

Promotional campaigns are activities and programs done to entice buyers and make them patronize you.

If I run a drink producing outfit, I could come up with a promotional sales campaign for wholesalers to buy ten packs and get one pack free. If my products are sealed can put coupons to be won in the seal, and run advert of people winning fabulous prizes when they buy my products, whereas not every buyer will win the big stuffs, some will be lucky to win big, some will win consolation prizes. A movie cinema may declare free show to those who could prove or provide up to six or more past tickets.

If I run a snack and drink shop, I can run a quiz program for teens let's say on weekends, and offer snacks to winners, in the end they tend to buy drinks to take this snacks, its will definitely increase my drink sale that weekend, beyond that weekend the program will be a talk of the town among teens and they will definitely stick around my shop to keep me encouraged or get informed about the next program of such.

Marketing to achieve great sales is not just about being skillful, entertaining to people, knowledgeable about business but also involves being cunning.

Marketing actually unearth and make buyers active, brand on the other hand turns them to loyal or satisfied customers. The satisfaction derived from product and services also enable clients become preachers and advocates authenticating the quality of your services.

Branding is that aspect of marketing that encompasses all the processes of identifying, recognizing and satisfying customers by meeting their needs and wants through the sale of products and services and ensuring being outstanding than other players in competition, in a consistent and timely manner. *One top secret about Marketing that enhances sales is Branding.*

We will be back on branding, meanwhile let's consider the P's of Marketing.

The first **P** is **Product**: without a product, there can't be a business not to talk of marketing, marketing involves ensuring everything possible is done to ensure the purchase of a product from its manufacturer, seller or supplier. Product comes with a well designed package that makes it attractive to the buyer. Whatever any organization releases from its process as an output is that product it sells, simply the value they exchange for money.

All products have **Prices**, there must be a price tag on every value a firm gives out, it could involve discount and allowances over wholesale or retail purchases, it must be noted that price should be commensurate with the perceived value of every offer, or else buyer will turn to competitors in choosing their products.

Place stands for distribution, i.e. the strategy the organization employs to ensure availability and accessibility of their product by targeted customers in the market, this practically involves relationship with the middlemen;

transporters, wholesalers, retailers and other market facilitators, such that products arrive in time in the market.

Promotion involves the activities embarked by the organization in order to communicate their product and its advantages to the society, the customers and market facilitators as to why they should pick their product above that of the competitors.

It's not enough to know the four P's of marketing; you should not just practice the old style of business engagements the same way we were taught back then in business colleges. Situations are different now, there are new turns and diverse perspective to various things recently, different situation requires different attention. Though most of these elements remain with the same names and utility but there is a great need for entrepreneurs to explore and express their creativity by tweaking these business principles to suit the present time and needs.

Other means of Tweaking your Marketing Ps to ensure productivity achieve massive sales.

- Invest in advertisement

-

- Run sales promotion program with incentives

-

- Referral system with incentive will also go a long way...it's tested and confirmed, ask the MLM guys.

-

- Sales promotion

-

- Quoting customer's testimonials (reviews).

-

Marketing your business for success requires engaging in activities that will be remembered by all who sees them and not forgotten by all ears who hear of it.

It's evidently essential to brand your product as it creates awareness and identity as well as helping to build reputation of this product and organization.

The basic purpose of branding strategy is to create product and services that are easily distinguished from that of the competitors, by means of which the number of substitutes in the marketplace is reduced. When you achieve high brand equity through brand differentiation, price elasticity of your product or service kind demand becomes low, thereby giving your organization the opportunity to raise rate or price which transcends to improvement in profitability.

The efficiency of branding as one of the most important aspect of a business gives a major edge in an increasingly competitive markets.

You may wonder how branding affects our business when put in place and what negative impact it may have when absent.

Branding is what differentiates your products from others. Whatever branding intuition you have got, it emanated from whom you are and how you want to be seen or known. Branding interprets to buyers what they should expect from your products and services- you can never represent two sides e.g. high and low price at the same time; that will definitely ruin the successful sale of any product.

Every Brand should have a unique logo, a well designed packaging as well as promotional materials. The whole has become a global village with the advent of internet, therefore if your business does not have a website yet, you may not be in for expansion and being known far and beyond.

Simple steps to effective branding

- **You need a great and unique logo.** Place it everywhere.

-

- **Identify and pen down your brand messaging.** There should be key messages to be communicated often about your brand.

-

- **Integrate your brand.** Every aspect of business should have a way it represent your brand, right from phones usage with clients, wearing of branded attires to sales calls oriented meetings or appointments as well as e-mail signature, among many others.

-

- **Create a "voice" for your company that reflects your brand.** Communication ethics that best suits your brand should be adopted.

-

- **Taglines are memorable.** Statements that capture the essence of your products become irreplaceable and memorable in the heart of people.

-

- **Ensure to deliver promises.** Inability to deliver brand promises will break the chain of referrals, negative comments spreads faster take note.

-

- **Be consistent.** Consistency is key in establishing a brand in the heart of everyone.

•

CHAPTER SEVEN

EFFECT OF GOOD CUSTOMER RELATIONS ON SALES

Quite a number of people do not understand the magic behind customer care, they just get workers recruited into that unit based on university education and fluency in talking or giving responses to sales related questions.

It takes deep reasoning to understand how to equip a customer service unit; Customer service is beyond that having personnel with high education.

As an employer you need to understand the kind of personality that will magnetize sales, when he or she is drafted to the customer service unit, you need the insight to discern what you need for your kind of products or services.

A customer service personnel must be knowledgeable about the products he or she sells, should know how to convince clients with the merits over the weakness of his or her products. Employing people in this unit requires testing their ability on how to convince a buyer to buy amidst competition even with the weakness of your own products.

A customer service personnel must be a friendly/jovial person, must be a smiling person, should be one who can penetrate into customers heart with smiles and words friendliness.

A customer service personality must have a dressing sense: dressing commands respect, dressing attracts the right person. A customer service personnel do not necessarily need to dress in a seductive way.(though sometimes that is key).

Then as an employer you need ladies who can go the extra mile to take charge of units as such for your organization. *(Employees are to use their discretion here not to get into a jeopardy situation).*

This situation is well understood and practiced in fuel filling stations, financial services institution that work more on deposit and the likes.

A business that deals with specific gender items are best marketed by the opposite gender. *TRUST ME!*

Imagine a well looking and handsome young man selling bra, it may look funny, but believe me, lots of female buyers will troop to that shop to purchase. So many other examples should flow into your mind now.

I guess you would have witnessed lots of business transactions, if you are above twenty year old or more, counting them may number up to millions.

Do I need to think if you have ever had business transactions done personally? I guess no, why?

This eBook is specially made for business owners.

Back to the point of discussion, Customer relations is one of the major impetuses behind SALES.

It's essential to maintain a good relationship in every area of life, yes! Even in business relationship which is the main concern of this eBook.

A cordial relationship keeps and breeds a healthy situation; the sleekness of transactional activities can only be achieved with smooth relationship.

Competition in business has increased in recent years, a lot of people are now in business, this singular reason has made sales get dispersed: It's now a struggle of between all active sellers....Yeah it's almost normal, only few sellers make real and substantial sales. These few sellers comprises of the lucky ones and those who understands the secrets behind making sales.

In view of this, I guess you now understand the essence of being friendly to customers when you are a seller.

TWO SHORT BEAUTIFUL STORY TO LEARN FROM

1. *"A young man was posted to work in an unfamiliar city, after settling in, he filled his gas cylinder in different places for a while because he wasn't satisfied as the gas finishes way before scheduled time until he came across a station that impressed him not only for the service rendered but for their good customer relations; coming into the station, he was offered help in carrying his cylinder by a one of the station workers, he was offered a sit and asked to pick from a soft drink menu what he should be offered, he smiled and said immediately, sorry, I don't have extra cash to buy any other thing, the sales person smiled back saying sir, everything on the menu is free, its one drink for each customer. The*

young man coming from under the intense sun was more than happy and impressed, he also noted that the gas didn't finish before supposed time, he went back to the gas station weeks later and the treatment was the same, he never changed his gas filling station all the years he spent in that city referring everyone of his colleagues and friends both far and near to the station to fill their cylinders also in the same place."

2.

3. *A lady who often purchased coffee from a tea/coffee outlet was amazed when she got a note that followed her order after a while that she didn't come*

around, the note reads *"WOW, Hi, Johanna! It's so lovely to see your name come up! We miss you dearly, we are glad that you're doing great"*. *The lady was more than satisfied, while narrating her experience she said, this isn't something I normally get from other places I shop, because of this, they will always be one of my important go to places.*

4.

Two cogent things happened in our stories, there was *Customer Satisfaction* in one and the other is a very good example of customer retention which is only achievable when there is *Customer's Loyalty*.

Customer's satisfaction happens when purchased products and or services meets or exceeds expectation of the customer, this is a basic factor that contributes and determines the success or failure of any business. When customer's satisfaction is met, it does not only guarantee the happiness and fulfillment of the customer but also ensures customers go on advertising your services and products on your behalf, this in line improves sales and increases revenue.

Customer's loyalty stems from customers satisfaction but it involves much more; a natural man wants convenient, wants easy, and wants stress free or cheap things. A customer could be satisfied by the product and services rendered by *outlet A* that she goes on to even recommend it to others but when he/she finds another place that offers same services and the expectations are met or surpassed at lesser stress, say it's closer to resident or place of need, it's easier to access or its cheaper to buy, there's all possibility that its one customer loss for *outlet A.*

To retain customers even in the most competitive market situation, achieving customer loyalty is key.

A renowned business trainer, Jeffery Gitomer once said *"Customer's satisfaction is worthless... Customer's Loyalty is priceless".*

SO, HOW DO WE ACHIEVE CUSTOMER LOYALTY?

Customer's Satisfaction

Customer loyalty starts from the point of first satisfying clients' overtime; these clients tend to reminisce on their first or previous experience with the seller. This will make them go extra mile with sacrifices on purchasing from a preferred seller irrespective of distance, price or any other factor. There's no customer retention plan that will work without first the presentation of expected services; ensure quality products, show respect, foster a friendly atmosphere, appreciation of customers and provision of a listening ear to customers, as well as being responsive to them.

Build Customer Relationship

Relationship is that one factor that bonds or breaks two separate entities. In relation to business, identify your semi-regular and regular clients, try to show care for their personal life by getting a reasonable degree closer, do well to remember your last discussions especially with regards their needs. *(Say a woman always come to buy goods with her son, if she has been coming for a while without him, ask about the son, show care beyond the business relationship).*

Check on them when they are not around or did not come around to make purchase. Some of them travel far, leaving sellers around them to purchase from you.

Building customer relationship starts from showing respect to all clients irrespective of their status, age or gender. Massaging clients' ego will never be forgotten in a hurry, humans want to be accorded respect always. A customer that was accorded respect will definitely show up, when this happen repeatedly, **LOYALTY** is already achieved.

CUSTOMER LOYALTY IS BUILT ON COMMUNICATION: everyone likes to be listened to; same trend happens when it involves patronage on business issues. Sellers need to be attentive to what their clients have to say, there is need to create a platform for easy communication, listen and request for feedbacks, send messages to mails and contacts, asking questions from each customer with whatever seems particular to them.

Preferential Treatment

Sometimes you force few people to become loyal, once you notice them in your outlet frequently or a few times, you can give them a reasonable discount, or it could just be the special offering of seat or the meet and greet system with help to skip the long lines, etc. If they want to make purchase when they have less cash with them, give them the grace of making payment flexibly while they go with the goods based on trust. All these will convince new customers to stick around and enjoy same benefits.

Please do this with utmost care, don't risk too much, not all persons can be trusted.

Give incentives and Merchandise

Incentives and merchandise such as organization free printed designed T-shirts, customized children play things and writing materials, etc. keeps customers loyal and coming back even when they could get a satisfactory service somewhere else.

Good customer relation is essential for gaining and keeping customers. It motivates and encourages customer to go the extra mile in order to continually enjoy the quality services rendered which consequentially translate in an improved sales and increase in revenue.

SUCCESS BELONGS TO ACTION TAKERS-

In my learning days, I often feel life happens anyhow, especially when I first came across whatever will be will be,

Deep down my heart I hate that statement with perfect hatred, owing that it had robbed many of the opportunities that would have changed their wellbeing and generation forever.

As much as more it's not advisable to rush things but think deeply and rationally, asking questions on areas not clear, in same vein slackness or non-prompt actions are more than detrimental.

Fear of the unknown has kept quite a lot of talents under the carpet while many others die with great potentials, just because they never give a trial.

There is no harm in trying; trying out something without success will only teach you to try a better method than that which you first tried.

In this piece I would be compiling the summary f this whole eBook.

First, take step and try out that business, that's the only means you can get independent income with the most flexible timing.

Have you considered the purpose of you business existence and participation or operations?

Finding out the right model to work with will be more than perfect. Identify which company you will make your role model, improve on their strengths and work on how their weakness can be our strengths also.

You need to also set goals, high and crazy goals, so if you don't meet up, you still fall on a very high line. You need to imagine where you want to be as a businessman in the next one, two, five or ten years; then you work towards it, planning with the resources you have at hand and calculate how to get those resources needed to achieve your objectives.

Learn how to get the best out of your staff, employee gives their best when treated well, on the other hand some staff work more when you criticize them and deprived them of some benefits. These schools of thought have helped many and have also ruined many. You need to first observe what work for you, your society or organization.

Don't forget to present value, if your products and services are valuable and irreplaceable, clients will find you to that nook and cranny where you operate.

Meanwhile don't forget you may also need a show room in the metropolitan areas where people can see a gallery of hat you can offer and make request for your products. Home delivery is always a boom to the busy customers, many would even appreciate ordering online while you deliver to their home, at this point you need a website for online presence.

Get a stunning and user friendly website, SEO will go a long way, find my business on goggle will bring in clients you never expect as well as press releases and frequent social media postings.

Here we go, dedicate yourself to develop your marketing skills, erase every form of impossibility, make prospecting clients your daily routine, those who promise to check back on you, why not do cold calling, it means you need to start getting phone numbers and emails of prospects and leads.

These phone numbers can be useful for cold calling, broadcast message through you 'whatsapp business software', you can send bulk SMS, email blast and the likes.

Whatsapp Business enables you have a business presence on Whatsapp which is commonly seen on virtually all Phones in recent times.

Sending an enticing sales letter to thousands of email recipients would bring in clients in their multitude; imagine converting hundred out of every two thousand email lead to regular clients, repeating this overtime will blast your sales record.

Hey, I hope you haven't forgot your customer retention skills, you need to work on how you relate with your customers, you need the money in their pocket, therefore you only duty is to massage their ego and make them derive satisfaction from you, overtime they trust you more than any other seller even when you have a higher price or change location.

TAKE IT OUTSIDE... Permit me share these examples, they are from local backgrounds but they should inspire you.

I had the opportunity to visit a developing country in Africa, on this fateful day I was in one of the major markets and I saw things that would stick to my head forever.

I saw people whose outlets are in the inner market having sales spy at the market entrance asking people if they want some kind of products and telling them they could get those products with wonderful features and discount if they patronize their stores....this is amazing, I first thought selfishness for sales would have inspired this until I saw the level of competition and immediately I understood why it is necessary to take actions.

The market has variety of goods on sale by sellers, there was the fabric section, shoe section, foods in different categories and all that, something else baffles me: A yam-flour seller, who moves around to the fabric and other products section to advertise how good her yam-flour is, they then place order, she goes ahead to sell to fellow market sellers who are into other products other than foodstuff, yet she still sells to buyers who primarily come to the market to buy, after a brief discussion with her, I learnt she own three houses in the metropolis.

Another intriguing one is a PHD holder who got no job and recruits talented fashion designers; he buys different materials and gets these boys to sew them while he takes these clothes to offices and people of high class. His business is really a boom.

In summary, I urge you to take step, take risk, and take action.

www.ingramcontent.com/pod-product-compliance
Lightning Source LLC
Chambersburg PA
CBHW020921180526
45163CB00007B/2830